THY KINGDOM COME

Common Worship

Daily Prayer for
Thy Kingdom Come

**Morning, Evening, Day and Night Prayer
from Ascension to Pentecost**

CHURCH HOUSE
PUBLISHING

Published by Church House Publishing
Church House, Great Smith Street, London SW1P 3AZ
www.chpublishing.co.uk

Copyright © The Archbishops' Council 2019

First published 2019

978-0-7151-2359-1 (PB)
978-0-7151-2365-2 (10 Pack)
978-0-7151-2366-9 (50 Pack)

Designed by www.stellaedwards.com
Printed in the UK by Ashford Colour Press Ltd

Contents

INTRODUCTION   **4**

MORNING PRAYER   **5**
from the day after Ascension Day until the Day of Pentecost

EVENING PRAYER   **13**
from the day after Ascension Day until the Day of Pentecost

PRAYER DURING THE DAY   **22**
from Ascension Day until the Day of Pentecost

NIGHT PRAYER   **28**
from Ascension Day until the Day of Pentecost

PSALMS, READINGS AND PRAYERS   **36**
for Thy Kingdom Come

   Table of Lectionary psalms   **38**

   Table of Lectionary readings   **39**

   Short readings from Prayer During the Day   **40**

   Readings on the theme of Evangelism and Discipleship   **43**

   Praying for your Five during Thy Kingdom Come   **45**

   A form of intercession   **46**

   Authorization and acknowledgements   **47**

THE LORD'S PRAYER   **48**

Introduction

During *Thy Kingdom Come*, you are invited to discover new habits and ways of praying to God, that those whom you know might come to know Jesus.

From the earliest days of the Church, people have gathered together to praise God and to pray for salvation through his Son. The services in this booklet form part of what is sometimes known as the 'Daily Office', a form of worship and prayer which can be used by individuals or in groups as a structure for praise and petition. It is drawn from Common Worship, one of the worship resources of the Church of England.

Whether you are new to 'structured' prayer or an old hand, you are invited to try praying with us for the period between Ascension and Pentecost. We hope you may find in it a spiritual rhythm which will nourish your heart and keep prayer on your lips, enabling you to become part of a global wave of prayer. That rhythm might take the form of saying both Morning Prayer and Evening Prayer. Or you might start with just Prayer During the Day – suitable for any time of day – followed, perhaps, by Night Prayer.

HOW TO USE THIS BOOKLET

You can read what follows out loud, or to yourself. You can pray by yourself or in a group. When in a group, everyone can say the words in **bold type**.

You can choose to say or sing the psalms and songs together or to choose someone to speak and others to listen. A diamond ♦ marks the mid-point in each psalm verse, at which point some people follow the custom of taking a pause.

One psalm is included in each order of service, and a pattern of psalms for use at Morning and Evening Prayer can be found on page 38. Similarly, one short Bible reading is included within each service. Further short readings are included on pages 40 to 44, or you might want to follow the table of readings on page 39.

In the Prayers, you can pray out loud or silently whether by yourself or in a group. You can pray in your own words – perhaps following the daily themes on page 45 – or use the ones suggested on page 46.

MORNING
PRAYER

THY KINGDOM COME

FROM THE DAY AFTER ASCENSION DAY
UNTIL THE DAY OF PENTECOST

Preparation

O Lord, open our lips
All **and our mouth shall proclaim your praise.**

Send your Holy Spirit upon us,
All **and clothe us with power from on high. Alleluia.**

Blessed are you, creator God,
to you be praise and glory for ever.
As your Spirit moved over the face of the waters
bringing light and life to your creation,
pour out your Spirit on us today
that we may walk as children of light
and by your grace reveal your presence.
Blessed be God, Father, Son and Holy Spirit.
All **Blessed be God for ever.**

The night has passed, and the day lies open before us;
let us pray with one heart and mind.

Silence is kept.

As we rejoice in the gift of this new day,
so may the light of your presence, O God,
set our hearts on fire with love for you;
now and for ever.
All **Amen.**

The Word of God

PSALMODY

The following, or another psalm from the table on page 38, is said.

PSALM 46

1 God is our refuge and strength, ♦
a very present help in trouble;

2 Therefore we will not fear, though the earth be moved, ♦
and though the mountains tremble in the heart of the sea;

3 Though the waters rage and swell, ♦
and though the mountains quake at the towering seas.

4 There is a river whose streams make glad the city of God, ♦
the holy place of the dwelling of the Most High.

5 God is in the midst of her;
    therefore shall she not be removed; ♦
God shall help her at the break of day.

6 The nations are in uproar and the kingdoms are shaken, ♦
but God utters his voice and the earth shall melt away.

7 *The Lord of hosts is with us;* ♦
the God of Jacob is our stronghold.

8 Come and behold the works of the Lord, ♦
what destruction he has wrought upon the earth.

9 He makes wars to cease in all the world; ♦
he shatters the bow and snaps the spear
    and burns the chariots in the fire.

10 'Be still, and know that I am God; ♦
I will be exalted among the nations;
    I will be exalted in the earth.'

11 *The Lord of hosts is with us;* ♦
the God of Jacob is our stronghold.

God of Jacob,
when the earth shakes
and the nations are in uproar,
speak, and let the storm be still;
through Jesus Christ our Lord.

The psalm may end with

All **Glory to the Father and to the Son**
and to the Holy Spirit;
as it was in the beginning is now
and shall be for ever. Amen.

If there are two Scripture readings, the first may be read
here, or both may be read after the canticle.

CANTICLE

Refrain:

All **The Spirit of God fills the whole world. Alleluia.**

1   I will take you from the nations, ♦
    and gather you from all the countries.

2   I will sprinkle clean water upon you, ♦
    and you shall be clean from all your uncleannesses.

3   A new heart I will give you, ♦
    and put a new spirit within you,

4   And I will remove from your body the heart of stone ♦
    and give you a heart of flesh.

5   You shall be my people, ♦
    and I will be your God.   *Ezekiel 36.24-26,28b*

All **Glory to the Father and to the Son**
and to the Holy Spirit;
as it was in the beginning is now
and shall be for ever. Amen.

All **The Spirit of God fills the whole world. Alleluia.**

SCRIPTURE READING

One or more readings are read – either the following
passage, or one or more from the cycles on pages 39–44.

Have you not known? Have you not heard? The Lord is the
everlasting God, the Creator of the ends of the earth. He does
not faint or grow weary; his understanding is unsearchable.
He gives power to the faint, and strengthens the powerless.
Even youths will faint and be weary, and the young will fall
exhausted; but those who wait for the Lord shall renew their
strength, they shall mount up with wings like eagles, they
shall run and not be weary, they shall walk and not faint.

Isaiah 40.28-end

The reading(s) may be followed by a time of silence.

Come, Holy Spirit, fill the hearts of your people
All **and kindle in us the fire of your love.**

All who are led by the Spirit of God
are children of God and fellow-heirs with Christ.
All **Come, Holy Spirit, fill the hearts of your people.**

Renew the face of your creation, Lord,
pouring on us the gifts of your Spirit,
All **and kindle in us the fire of your love.**

For the creation waits with eager longing
for the glorious liberty of the children of God.
All **Come, Holy Spirit, fill the hearts of your people**
and kindle in us the fire of your love.   *cf Romans 8*

GOSPEL CANTICLE

The Benedictus (The Song of Zechariah) is said

Refrain

All **Christ has gone up on high
and has led captivity captive. Alleluia.**

1   Blessed be the Lord the God of Israel, ♦
    who has come to his people and set them free.

2   He has raised up for us a mighty Saviour, ♦
    born of the house of his servant David.

3   Through his holy prophets God promised of old ♦
    to save us from our enemies,
        from the hands of all that hate us,

4   To show mercy to our ancestors, ♦
    and to remember his holy covenant.

5   This was the oath God swore to our father Abraham: ♦
    to set us free from the hands of our enemies,

6   Free to worship him without fear, ♦
    holy and righteous in his sight
        all the days of our life.

7   And you, child, shall be called the prophet of the Most High, ♦
    for you will go before the Lord to prepare his way,

8   To give his people knowledge of salvation ♦
    by the forgiveness of all their sins.

9   In the tender compassion of our God ♦
    the dawn from on high shall break upon us,

10 To shine on those who dwell in darkness
        and the shadow of death, ♦
    and to guide our feet into the way of peace.

Luke 1.68-79

All **Glory to the Father and to the Son**
and to the Holy Spirit;
as it was in the beginning is now
and shall be for ever. Amen.

All **Christ has gone up on high**
and has led captivity captive. Alleluia.

Prayers

Intercessions are offered
- *for the day and its tasks*
- *for the world and its needs*
- *for the Church and her life*

*Intercessions may include Praying for your Five (page 45)
and/or the form of prayer on page 46.*

These responses may be used

Lord, in your mercy   *(or)*   Lord, hear us.
hear our prayer.   **Lord, graciously hear us.**

Silence may be kept.

*The Collect for Thy Kingdom Come or another suitable
Collect is said:*

Almighty God,
your ascended Son has sent us into the world
to preach the good news of your kingdom:
inspire us with your Spirit
and fill our hearts with the fire of your love,
that all who hear your Word
may be drawn to you,
through Jesus Christ our Lord.

All **Amen.**   *Collect for Thy Kingdom Come*

(or)

O God the King of glory,
you have exalted your only Son Jesus Christ
with great triumph to your kingdom in heaven:
we beseech you, leave us not comfortless,
but send your Holy Spirit to strengthen us
and exalt us to the place where our Saviour Christ
   is gone before,
who is alive and reigns with you,
in the unity of the Holy Spirit,
one God, now and for ever.

All **Amen.**

The Lord's Prayer is said

Being made one by the power of the Spirit,
as our Saviour taught us, so we pray

All **Our Father in heaven …**   *(see back page)*

(or)

Being made one by the power of the Spirit,
let us pray with confidence as our Saviour has taught us

All **Our Father, who art in heaven …**   *(see back page)*

The Conclusion

May the Spirit kindle in us the fire of God's love.

All **Amen.**

Let us bless the Lord. Alleluia, alleluia.

All **Thanks be to God. Alleluia, alleluia.**

EVENING PRAYER

FROM THE DAY AFTER ASCENSION DAY
UNTIL THE DAY OF PENTECOST

THY KINGDOM COME

Preparation

O God, make speed to save us.
All **O Lord, make haste to help us.**

Send your Holy Spirit upon us,
All **and clothe us with power from on high. Alleluia.**

1   Bless the Lord, O my soul. ♦
    O Lord my God, how excellent is your greatness!

2   You are clothed with majesty and honour, ♦
    wrapped in light as in a garment.

3   The sun knows the time for its setting. ♦
    You make darkness that it may be night.

4   O Lord, how manifold are your works! ♦
    In wisdom you have made them all;
        the earth is full of your creatures.

5   When you send forth your spirit, they are created, ♦
    and you renew the face of the earth.

6   May the glory of the Lord endure for ever; ♦
    may the Lord rejoice in his works;

7   I will sing to the Lord as long as I live; ♦
    I will make music to my God while I have my being.

Psalm 104.1,2,21b,22a,26,32,33,35

All **Glory to the Father and to the Son**
    and to the Holy Spirit;
    as it was in the beginning is now
    and shall be for ever. Amen.

That this evening may be holy, good and peaceful,
let us pray with one heart and mind.

Silence is kept.

As our evening prayer rises before you, O God,
so may your mercy come down upon us
to cleanse our hearts
and set us free to sing your praise
now and for ever.

All **Amen.**

The Word of God

PSALMODY

The following, or another psalm from the table on page 38, is said.

PSALM 48

Refrain: **We have waited on your loving-kindness, O God.**

1 Great is the Lord and highly to be praised, ✦
  in the city of our God.

2 His holy mountain is fair and lifted high, ✦
  the joy of all the earth.

3 On Mount Zion, the divine dwelling place, ✦
  stands the city of the great king.

4 In her palaces God has shown himself ✦
  to be a sure refuge.

5 For behold, the kings of the earth assembled ✦
  and swept forward together.

6 They saw, and were dumbfounded; ✦
  dismayed, they fled in terror.

7 Trembling seized them there;
    they writhed like a woman in labour, ✦
  as when the east wind shatters the ships of Tarshish.

8   As we had heard, so have we seen
      in the city of the Lord of hosts, the city of our God: ♦
  God has established her for ever.

9   We have waited on your loving-kindness, O God, ♦
  in the midst of your temple.

10 As with your name, O God,
      so your praise reaches to the ends of the earth; ♦
  your right hand is full of justice.

11 Let Mount Zion rejoice and the daughters of Judah be glad, ♦
  because of your judgements, O Lord.

12 Walk about Zion and go round about her;
      count all her towers; ♦
  consider well her bulwarks; pass through her citadels,

13 That you may tell those who come after
      that such is our God for ever and ever. ♦
  It is he that shall be our guide for evermore.

Refrain: **We have waited on your loving-kindness, O God.**

Father of lights,
raise us with Christ to your eternal city,
that, with kings and nations,
we may wait in the midst of your temple
and see your glory for ever and ever.

The psalm may end with

All **Glory to the Father and to the Son**
and to the Holy Spirit;
as it was in the beginning is now
and shall be for ever. Amen.

If there are two Scripture readings, the first may be read
here, or both may be read after the canticle.

CANTICLE

A Song of God's Children may be said

Refrain:

All **The Spirit of the Father,**
who raised Christ Jesus from the dead,
gives life to the people of God. Alleluia.

1   The law of the Spirit of life in Christ Jesus ♦
    has set us free from the law of sin and death.

2   All who are led by the Spirit of God are children of God; ♦
    for we have received the Spirit that enables us to cry,
       'Abba, Father'.

3   The Spirit himself bears witness that we are children of God ♦
    and if God's children, then heirs of God;

4   If heirs of God, then fellow-heirs with Christ; ♦
    since we suffer with him now,
       that we may be glorified with him.

5   These sufferings that we now endure ♦
    are not worth comparing to the glory that shall be revealed.

6   For the creation waits with eager longing ♦
    for the revealing of the children of God.

Romans 8.2,14,15b-19

All **Glory to the Father and to the Son**
    and to the Holy Spirit;
    as it was in the beginning is now
    and shall be for ever. Amen.

All **The Spirit of the Father,**
    who raised Christ Jesus from the dead,
    gives life to the people of God. Alleluia.

SCRIPTURE READING

*One or more readings are read – either the following
passage, or one or more from the cycles on pages 39–44.*

The Lord is the Spirit, and where the Spirit of the Lord is,
there is freedom. And all of us, with unveiled faces, seeing
the glory of the Lord as though reflected in a mirror,
are being transformed into the same image from one
degree of glory to another; for this comes from the Lord,
the Spirit. *2 Corinthians 3.17,18*

The reading(s) may be followed by a time of silence.

*A suitable song or chant, or a responsory in this or
another form, may follow*

When you send forth your Spirit, we are created;
you renew the face of the earth.

All **When you send forth your Spirit, we are created;
you renew the face of the earth.**

O Lord, how manifold are your works;
in wisdom you have made them all.

All **You renew the face of the earth.**

Glory to the Father and to the Son
and to the Holy Spirit.

All **When you send forth your Spirit, we are created;
you renew the face of the earth.** *from Psalm 104*

GOSPEL CANTICLE

The Magnificat (The Song of Mary) is said

Refrain:

All **How excellent is your name in all the world,**
you have set your glory above the heavens. Alleluia.

1   My soul proclaims the greatness of the Lord,
      my spirit rejoices in God my Saviour; ♦
    he has looked with favour on his lowly servant.

2   From this day all generations will call me blessed; ♦
    the Almighty has done great things for me
      and holy is his name.

3   He has mercy on those who fear him, ♦
    from generation to generation.

4   He has shown strength with his arm ♦
    and has scattered the proud in their conceit,

5   Casting down the mighty from their thrones ♦
    and lifting up the lowly.

6   He has filled the hungry with good things ♦
    and sent the rich away empty.

7   He has come to the aid of his servant Israel, ♦
    to remember his promise of mercy,

8   The promise made to our ancestors, ♦
    to Abraham and his children for ever.   *Luke 1.46-55*

All **Glory to the Father and to the Son**
    and to the Holy Spirit;
    as it was in the beginning is now
    and shall be for ever. Amen.

All **How excellent is your name in all the world,**
    you have set your glory above the heavens. Alleluia.

Prayers

Thanksgiving may be made for the day.

Intercessions are offered
- *for peace*
- *for individuals and their needs*

Intercessions may include Praying for your Five (page 45) and/or the form of prayer on page 46.

These responses may be used

Lord, in your mercy   *(or)*   Lord, hear us.
hear our prayer.   **Lord, graciously hear us.**

Silence may be kept.

The Collect for Thy Kingdom Come or another suitable Collect is said:

Almighty God,
your ascended Son has sent us into the world
to preach the good news of your kingdom:
inspire us with your Spirit
and fill our hearts with the fire of your love,
that all who hear your Word
may be drawn to you,
through Jesus Christ our Lord.
All **Amen.**   *Collect for Thy Kingdom Come*

(or)

O God the King of glory,
you have exalted your only Son Jesus Christ
with great triumph to your kingdom in heaven:
we beseech you, leave us not comfortless,
but send your Holy Spirit to strengthen us
and exalt us to the place where our Saviour Christ
   is gone before,
who is alive and reigns with you,
in the unity of the Holy Spirit,
one God, now and for ever.

All **Amen.**

The Lord's Prayer is said

Being made one by the power of the Spirit,
as our Saviour taught us, so we pray

All **Our Father in heaven ...**   *(see back page)*

(or)

Being made one by the power of the Spirit,
let us pray with confidence as our Saviour has taught us

All **Our Father, who art in heaven ...**   *(see back page)*

The Conclusion

May the Spirit kindle in us the fire of God's love.

All **Amen.**

Let us bless the Lord. Alleluia, alleluia.

All **Thanks be to God. Alleluia, alleluia.**

PRAYER DURING THE DAY

FROM ASCENSION DAY
UNTIL THE DAY OF PENTECOST

THY KINGDOM COME

Preparation

O God, make speed to save us.
All **O Lord, make haste to help us.**

Gladden the soul of your servant,
All **for to you, O Lord, I lift up my soul**.

Psalm 86.4

Praise

A hymn, song, canticle, extempore praise or

Blessed are you, the God of our ancestors,
worthy to be praised and exalted for ever.

Blessed is your holy and glorious name,
worthy to be praised and exalted for ever.

Blessed are you, in your holy and glorious temple,
worthy to be praised and exalted for ever.

Blessed are you who look into the depths,
worthy to be praised and exalted for ever.

Blessed are you, enthroned on the cherubim,
worthy to be praised and exalted for ever.

Blessed are you on the throne of your kingdom,
worthy to be praised and exalted for ever.

Blessed are you in the heights of heaven,
worthy to be praised and exalted for ever.

The Song of the Three 29-34

The Word of God

PSALMODY

*Psalm 47 below may be read on Ascension Day
and on any day, or this daily cycle may be followed*

Sunday	Psalm 104.26-32	*Thursday*	Psalm 84
Monday	Psalm 21.1-7	*Friday*	Psalm 93
Tuesday	Psalm 29	*Saturday*	Psalm 98
Wednesday	Psalm 46		

PSALM 47

Refrain: **O sing praises to God, sing praises.**

1   Clap your hands together, all you peoples; ♦
    O sing to God with shouts of joy.

2   For the Lord Most High is to be feared; ♦
    he is the great King over all the earth.

3   He subdued the peoples under us ♦
    and the nations under our feet.

4   He has chosen our heritage for us, ♦
    the pride of Jacob, whom he loves.

5   God has gone up with a merry noise, ♦
    the Lord with the sound of the trumpet.

6   O sing praises to God, sing praises; ♦
    sing praises to our King, sing praises.

7   For God is the King of all the earth; ♦
    sing praises with all your skill.

8   God reigns over the nations; ♦
    God has taken his seat upon his holy throne.

9   The nobles of the peoples are gathered together ♦
    with the people of the God of Abraham.

10 For the powers of the earth belong to God ♦
    and he is very highly exalted.

Refrain: **O sing praises to God, sing praises.**

> *As Christ was raised by your glory, O Father,*
> *so may we be raised to new life*
> *and rejoice to be called your children,*
> *both now and for ever.*

The psalm may end with

All **Glory to the Father and to the Son**
    and to the Holy Spirit;
    as it was in the beginning is now
    and shall be for ever. Amen.

SHORT READINGS

Either a short reading from the daily cycle on pages 40–42,
or

Christ did not enter a sanctuary made by human hands,
a mere copy of the true one, but he entered into heaven
itself, now to appear in the presence of God on our behalf.

Hebrews 9.24

Response

Silence, study, song, or words from Scripture, such as

Blessed are those who mourn,

All **for they will be comforted.**   *Matthew 5.4*

Prayers

Prayers may include these concerns:
- *God's royal priesthood, that it may be empowered by the Spirit*
- *Those who wait on God, that they may find renewal*
- *All people, that they may acknowledge the kingdom of the ascended Christ*
- *The earth, for productivity and for fruitful harvests*
- *All who are struggling with broken relationships*

Intercessions may include Praying for your Five (page 45) and/or the form of prayer on page 46.

The Collect for Thy Kingdom Come or another suitable Collect is said:

Almighty God,
your ascended Son has sent us into the world
to preach the good news of your kingdom:
inspire us with your Spirit
and fill our hearts with the fire of your love,
that all who hear your Word
may be drawn to you,
through Jesus Christ our Lord.

All **Amen.**   *Collect for Thy Kingdom Come*

(or)

O King enthroned on high,
Comforter and Spirit of truth,
you that are in all places and fill all things,
the treasury of blessings and the giver of life,
come and dwell with us,
cleanse us from every stain
and save our souls, O gracious one.

All **Amen.**   *an Orthodox prayer*

The Lord's Prayer is said

Being made one by the power of the Spirit,
as our Saviour taught us, so we pray

All **Our Father in heaven ...**   *(see back page)*

(or)

Being made one by the power of the Spirit,
let us pray with confidence as our Saviour has taught us

All **Our Father, who art in heaven ...**   *(see back page)*

The Conclusion

May the grace of the Holy Spirit enlighten our hearts
and minds.

All **Alleluia. Amen.**

NIGHT PRAYER

AN ORDER FOR NIGHT PRAYER
(COMPLINE)

THY KINGDOM COME

Preparation

The Lord almighty grant us a quiet night and a perfect end.

All **Amen.**

Our help is in the name of the Lord

All **who made heaven and earth.**

A period of silence for reflection on the past day may follow.

The following or other suitable words of penitence may be used

All **Most merciful God,**
we confess to you,
before the whole company of heaven and one another,
that we have sinned in thought, word and deed
and in what we have failed to do.
Forgive us our sins,
heal us by your Spirit
and raise us to new life in Christ. Amen.

O God, make speed to save us.

All **O Lord, make haste to help us.**

All **Glory to the Father and to the Son**
and to the Holy Spirit;
as it was in the beginning is now
and shall be for ever. Amen.
Alleluia.

The following or another suitable hymn may be sung

**Before the ending of the day,
Creator of the world, we pray
That you, with steadfast love, would keep
Your watch around us while we sleep.**

**From evil dreams defend our sight,
From fears and terrors of the night;
Tread underfoot our deadly foe
That we no sinful thought may know.**

**O Father, that we ask be done
Through Jesus Christ, your only Son;
And Holy Spirit, by whose breath
Our souls are raised to life from death.**

The Word of God

PSALMODY

PSALM 86

1   Incline your ear, O Lord, and answer me, ♦
  for I am poor and in misery.

2   Preserve my soul, for I am faithful; ♦
  save your servant, for I put my trust in you.

3   Be merciful to me, O Lord, for you are my God; ♦
  I call upon you all the day long.

4   Gladden the soul of your servant, ♦
  for to you, O Lord, I lift up my soul.

5   For you, Lord, are good and forgiving, ♦
  abounding in steadfast love to all who call upon you.

6   Give ear, O Lord, to my prayer ♦
  and listen to the voice of my supplication.

7   In the day of my distress I will call upon you, ♦
     for you will answer me.

8   Among the gods there is none like you, O Lord, ♦
     nor any works like yours.

9   All nations you have made shall come and worship you, O Lord, ♦
     and shall glorify your name.

10 For you are great and do wonderful things; ♦
     you alone are God.

11 Teach me your way, O Lord, and I will walk in your truth; ♦
     knit my heart to you, that I may fear your name.

12 I will thank you, O Lord my God, with all my heart, ♦
     and glorify your name for evermore;

13 For great is your steadfast love towards me, ♦
     for you have delivered my soul
        from the depths of the grave.

14 O God, the proud rise up against me
        and a ruthless horde seek after my life; ♦
     they have not set you before their eyes.

15 But you, Lord, are gracious and full of compassion, ♦
     slow to anger and full of kindness and truth.

16 Turn to me and have mercy upon me; ♦
     give your strength to your servant
        and save the child of your handmaid.

17 Show me a token of your favour,
        that those who hate me may see it and be ashamed; ♦
     because you, O Lord, have helped and comforted me.

All **Glory to the Father and to the Son**
     and to the Holy Spirit;
     as it was in the beginning is now
     and shall be for ever. Amen.

SCRIPTURE READING

The following short reading or another suitable passage is read

I will pour out my spirit on all flesh; your sons and your daughters shall prophesy. The old shall dream dreams and the young shall see visions.   *Joel 2.28*

The following responsory may be said

Into your hands, O Lord, I commend my spirit.
   Alleluia, alleluia.
All **Into your hands, O Lord, I commend my spirit.**
   Alleluia, alleluia.

For you have redeemed me, Lord God of truth.
All **Alleluia, alleluia.**

Glory to the Father and to the Son
and to the Holy Spirit.
All **Into your hands, O Lord, I commend my spirit.**
   Alleluia, alleluia.

Keep me as the apple of your eye.
All **Hide me under the shadow of your wings.**

GOSPEL CANTICLE

The Nunc dimittis (The Song of Simeon) is said or sung

All **Alleluia. The Holy Spirit, the Advocate, alleluia,**
shall teach you all things. Alleluia, alleluia.

1   Now, Lord, you let your servant go in peace: ♦
   your word has been fulfilled.

2   My own eyes have seen the salvation ♦
   which you have prepared in the sight of every people;

3   A light to reveal you to the nations ♦
     and the glory of your people Israel.   *Luke 2.29-32*

All **Glory to the Father and to the Son**
     and to the Holy Spirit;
     as it was in the beginning is now
     and shall be for ever. Amen.

All **Alleluia. The Holy Spirit, the Advocate, alleluia,**
     shall teach you all things. Alleluia, alleluia.

Prayers

Intercessions and thanksgivings may be offered here.

THE COLLECT

Silence may be kept.

Come, O Spirit of God,
and make within us your dwelling place and home.
May our darkness be dispelled by your light,
and our troubles calmed by your peace;
may all evil be redeemed by your love,
all pain transformed through the suffering of Christ,
and all dying glorified in his risen life.

All **Amen.**

The Lord's Prayer may be said (see back page).

The Conclusion

In peace we will lie down and sleep;
All **for you alone, Lord, make us dwell in safety.**

Abide with us, Lord Jesus,
All **for the night is at hand and the day is now past.**

As the night watch looks for the morning,
All **so do we look for you, O Christ.**

[Come with the dawning of the day
All **and make yourself known in the breaking of the bread.]**

May the Holy Spirit of God bless and sanctify us
so that we may be consecrated in the truth.
All **Amen.**

PSALMS,
READINGS
AND PRAYERS

DURING THY KINGDOM COME

Lectionary psalms and readings during Thy Kingdom Come

The psalms and readings printed in full in the text of the services in this booklet may be used on any day. However, you may wish to use a more varied selection of material during this period of prayer and preparation before Pentecost.

- You can use the special sequence of daily readings and psalms, which is suitable for either Morning Prayer or Evening Prayer. It is included on pages 38–39.

- Short readings for use at Prayer During the Day, or at another time, together with additional readings on the theme of evangelism and discipleship, are on pages 40–44.

- The official readings and psalms from the Lectionary for Morning and Evening Prayer are given in the tables on pages 38–39. Readings and psalms for the two Sundays follow a three-year pattern (Years A, B and C),* but those for all other days are the same each year.*

The dates of Ascension Day and Pentecost (Whit Sunday) and Lectionary years are as follows for 2019–2028:

Year	Ascension Day	Pentecost (Whit Sunday)	Lectionary
2019	30 May	9 June	Year C
2020	21 May	31 May	Year A
2021	13 May	23 May	Year B
2022	26 May	5 June	Year C
2023	18 May	28 May	Year A
2024	9 May	19 May	Year B
2025	29 May	8 June	Year C
2026	14 May	24 May	Year A
2027	6 May	16 May	Year B
2028	25 May	4 June	Year C

LECTIONARY PSALMS FOR MORNING AND EVENING PRAYER

Psalms printed in **bold** may be used as the sole psalm at that office.

Day	Morning Prayer	Evening Prayer
Ascension Day	Psalms 110, 150	Psalm 8
Friday after Ascension	Psalms 20, **81**	Psalm **145**
Saturday after Ascension	Psalms 21, **47**	Psalms 84, **85**
Sunday after Ascension **Year A**	Psalm 104.26–35	Psalm 47
Sunday after Ascension **Year B**	Psalm 76	Psalm 147.1–12
Sunday after Ascension **Year C**	Psalm 99	Psalm 68 [*or* 68.1–3, 18–19]
Monday	Psalms **93**, 96, 97	Psalm **18**
Tuesday	Psalms 98, **99**, 100	Psalm **68**
Wednesday	Psalms 2, **29**	Psalms 36, **46**
Thursday	Psalms **24**, 72	Psalm **139**
Friday	Psalms **28**, 30	Psalm **147**
Saturday	Psalms 42, **43**	Psalm **48**
Pentecost (Whit Sunday) **Year A**	Psalm 87	Psalms 67, 133
Pentecost (Whit Sunday) **Year B**	Psalm 145	Psalm 139.1–11 [13–18, 23–24]
Pentecost (Whit Sunday) **Year C**	Psalms 36.5–10; 150	Psalm 33.1–12

See the table on page 37 for dates of Ascension and Pentecost and Lectionary years.

LECTIONARY READINGS FOR USE
AT MORNING AND EVENING PRAYER

Ascension Day	**MP** Isaiah 52.7–end Hebrews 7. [11–25] 26–end	**EP** Song of the Three 29–37 *or* 2 Kings 2.1–15 Revelation 5
Friday after Ascension	Exodus 35.30–36.1	Galatians 5.13–end
Saturday after Ascension	Numbers 11.16–17, 24–29	1 Corinthians 2
Sunday after Ascension *Year A*	**MP** Isaiah 65.17–end Revelation 21.1–8	**EP** 2 Samuel 23.1–5 Ephesians 1.15–end
Sunday after Ascension *Year B*	**MP** Isaiah 14.3–15 Revelation 14.1–13	**EP** Isaiah 61 Luke 4.14–21
Sunday after Ascension *Year C*	**MP** Deuteronomy 34 Luke 24.44–end *or* Acts 1.1–8	**EP** Isaiah 44.1–8 Ephesians 4.7–16
Monday	Numbers 27.15–end	1 Corinthians 3
Tuesday	1 Samuel 10.1–10	1 Corinthians 12.1–13
Wednesday	1 Kings 19.1–18	Matthew 3.13–end
Thursday	Ezekiel 11.14–20	Matthew 9.35–10.20
Friday	Ezekiel 36.22–28	Matthew 12.22–32
Saturday	Micah 3.1–8 Ephesians 6.10–20	**EP** Deuteronomy 16.9–15 John 7.37–39
Pentecost (Whit Sunday) *Year A*	**MP** Genesis 11.1-9 Acts 10.34-end	**EP** Joel 2.21–end Acts 2.14–21 [22–38]
Pentecost (Whit Sunday) *Year B*	**MP** Isaiah 11.1–9 *or* Wisdom 7.15–23 [24–27] 1 Corinthians 12.4–13	**EP** Ezekiel 36.22–28 Acts 2.22–38
Pentecost (Whit Sunday) *Year C*	**MP** Isaiah 40.12–23 *or* Wisdom 9.9–17 1 Corinthians 2.6–end	**EP** Exodus 33.7–20 2 Corinthians 3.4–end

See the table on page 37 for dates of Ascension and Pentecost and Lectionary years.

SHORT READINGS FROM PRAYER DURING THE DAY

ASCENSION DAY OR ON ANY DAY AFTER ASCENSION

Christ did not enter a sanctuary made by human hands, a mere copy of the true one, but he entered into heaven itself, now to appear in the presence of God on our behalf.

Hebrews 9.24

FRIDAY AFTER ASCENSION

As it is, we do not yet see everything in subjection to human beings, but we do see Jesus, who for a little while was made lower than the angels, now crowned with glory and honour because of the suffering of death, so that by the grace of God he might taste death for everyone. It was fitting that God, for whom and through whom all things exist, in bringing many children to glory, should make the pioneer of their salvation perfect through sufferings.

Hebrews 2.8b-10

SATURDAY AFTER ASCENSION

I am convinced that neither death, nor life, nor angels, nor rulers, nor things present, nor things to come, nor powers, nor height, nor depth, nor anything else in all creation, will be able to separate us from the love of God in Christ Jesus our Lord.

Romans 8.38,39

SUNDAY AFTER ASCENSION

On the last day of the festival, the great day, while Jesus was standing there, he cried out, 'Let anyone who is thirsty come to me, and let the one who believes in me drink. As the scripture has said, "Out of the believer's heart shall flow rivers of living water."' Now he said this about the Spirit, which believers in him were to receive.

John 7.37-39a

MONDAY

Have you not known? Have you not heard? The Lord is the everlasting God, the Creator of the ends of the earth. He does not faint or grow weary; his understanding is unsearchable. He gives power to the faint, and strengthens the powerless. Even youths will faint and be weary, and the young will fall exhausted; but those who wait for the Lord shall renew their strength, they shall mount up with wings like eagles, they shall run and not be weary, they shall walk and not faint.

Isaiah 40.28-end

TUESDAY

Now there are varieties of gifts, but the same Spirit; and there are varieties of services, but the same Lord; and there are varieties of activities, but it is the same God who activates all of them in everyone. To each is given the manifestation of the Spirit for the common good.

I Corinthians 12.4-7

WEDNESDAY

I will pour out my spirit on all flesh; your sons and your daughters shall prophesy, your old men shall dream dreams, and your young men shall see visions. Even on the male and female slaves, in those days, I will pour out my spirit.

Joel 2.28,29

THURSDAY

Jesus said, 'Ask, and it will be given to you; search, and you will find; knock, and the door will be opened for you. For everyone who asks receives, and everyone who searches finds, and for everyone who knocks, the door will be opened. Is there anyone among you who, if your child asks for a fish, will give a snake instead of a fish? Or if the child asks for an egg, will give a scorpion? If you then, who are evil, know how to give good gifts to your children, how much more will the heavenly Father give the Holy Spirit to those who ask him!'

Luke 11.9-13

FRIDAY

In Christ every one of God's promises is a 'Yes'. For this reason it is through him that we say the 'Amen', to the glory of God. But it is God who establishes us with you in Christ and has anointed us, by putting his seal on us and giving us his Spirit in our hearts as a first instalment.

2 Corinthians 1.20-22

SATURDAY

The Lord is the Spirit, and where the Spirit of the Lord is, there is freedom. And all of us, with unveiled faces, seeing the glory of the Lord as though reflected in a mirror, are being transformed into the same image from one degree of glory to another; for this comes from the Lord, the Spirit.

2 Corinthians 3.17,18

THE DAY OF PENTECOST

Jesus said, 'Peace be with you. As the Father has sent me, so I send you.' When he had said this, he breathed on them and said to them, 'Receive the Holy Spirit.'

John 20.21,22

READINGS ON THE THEME OF EVANGELISM AND DISCIPLESHIP

And now the Lord says, who formed me in the womb to be his servant, to bring Jacob back to him, and that Israel might be gathered to him, for I am honoured in the sight of the Lord, and my God has become my strength – he says, 'It is too light a thing that you should be my servant to raise up the tribes of Jacob and to restore the survivors of Israel; I will give you as a light to the nations, that my salvation may reach to the end of the earth.'
Isaiah 49.5-6

Listen! Your sentinels lift up their voices, together they sing for joy; for in plain sight they see the return of the Lord to Zion. Break forth together into singing, you ruins of Jerusalem; for the Lord has comforted his people, he has redeemed Jerusalem.
Isaiah 52.8-9

Many nations shall come and say: 'Come, let us go up to the mountain of the Lord, to the house of the God of Jacob; that he may teach us his ways and that we may walk in his paths.' For out of Zion shall go forth instruction, and the word of the Lord from Jerusalem. He shall judge between many peoples, and shall arbitrate between strong nations far away; they shall beat their swords into ploughshares, and their spears into pruning-hooks; nation shall not lift up sword against nation, neither shall they learn war any more.
Micah 4.2-3

'While God has overlooked the times of human ignorance, now he commands all people everywhere to repent, because he has fixed a day on which he will have the world judged in righteousness by a man whom he has appointed, and of this he has given assurance to all by raising him from the dead.'
Acts 17.30-31

From now on, therefore, we regard no one from a human point of view; even though we once knew Christ from a human point of view, we know him no longer in that way. So if anyone is in Christ, there is a new creation: everything old has passed away; see, everything has become new!
2 Corinthians 5.16-17

So then you are no longer strangers and aliens, but you are citizens with the saints and also members of the household of God, built upon the foundation of the apostles and prophets, with Christ Jesus himself as the cornerstone. In him the whole structure is joined together and grows into a holy temple in the Lord.

Ephesians 2.19-21

Jesus said, 'You are the salt of the earth; but if salt has lost its taste, how can its saltiness be restored? It is no longer good for anything, but is thrown out and trampled under foot. You are the light of the world. A city built on a hill cannot be hidden. No one after lighting a lamp puts it under the bushel basket, but on the lampstand, and it gives light to all in the house. In the same way, let your light shine before others, so that they may see your good works and give glory to your Father in heaven.'

Matthew 5.13-16

Now the eleven disciples went to Galilee, to the mountain to which Jesus had directed them. When they saw him, they worshipped him; but some doubted. And Jesus came and said to them, 'All authority in heaven and on earth has been given to me. Go therefore and make disciples of all nations, baptizing them in the name of the Father and of the Son and of the Holy Spirit, and teaching them to obey everything that I have commanded you. And remember, I am with you always, to the end of the age.'

Matthew 28.16-end

Jesus said, 'Father, I desire that those also, whom you have given me, may be with me where I am, to see my glory, which you have given me because you loved me before the foundation of the world. Righteous Father, the world does not know you, but I know you; and these know that you have sent me. I made your name known to them, and I will make it known, so that the love with which you have loved me may be in them, and I in them.'

John 17.24-end

PRAYING FOR YOUR FIVE DURING THY KINGDOM COME

Thy Kingdom Come encourages every Christian to pray for five individuals so that they would know God's love for them in Christ.

ASCENSION DAY Jesus
Pray for your five friends to encounter Jesus in all his beauty, grace, challenge and love, that they might say with St Paul, 'For me, to live is Christ'.

FRIDAY AFTER ASCENSION Praise
Pray for your five to be woken up to all that they have already received from God in their lives, and all that he offers them in Christ, that they might praise him.

SATURDAY AFTER ASCENSION Thanks
Pray for your five to recognise the goodness of God in their lives, that they would turn to God in gratitude and trust.

SUNDAY AFTER ASCENSION Sorry
Pray for your five to be led by the Holy Spirit to understand the cost of God's love for them in Christ, that this great kindness would lead them to repentance.

MONDAY Offer
Pray for the Holy Spirit to bring an understanding of the life in all its fullness that will be theirs as your five put everything they have at the disposal of God.

TUESDAY Pray for
Pray for the oil of the Holy Spirit to pour into the lives of your five, as you pray for specific things they face.

WEDNESDAY Help
Pray for your five that they would know that they never have to face anything alone, but that in their need they would call on God for help.

THURSDAY Adore
Pray for the eyes of your five to be opened to all that Jesus offers them and that they would turn their faces to him and enjoy the warmth of his love.

FRIDAY Celebrate
Pray for yourself and those others the Lord sends to help show your five their route home to God, that they would know the loving father running to greet them.

SATURDAY Silence
Pray for the Holy Spirit to engrave on your heart the desires of heaven for your five.

THE DAY OF PENTECOST Thy Kingdom Come
Pray 'Come Holy Spirit' for your five friends, that they may joyfully enter the Kingdom of God and find themselves used by God to pray and act 'Thy Kingdom Come'.

A form of intercession

Prayers during Ascension to Pentecost may include the following concerns from the seasonal cycle in Common Worship: Daily Prayer

- *God's royal priesthood, for empowerment by the Spirit*
- *Those who wait on God, that they may find renewal*
- *All people, that they may acknowledge the kingdom of the ascended Christ*
- *The earth, for productivity and for fruitful harvests*
- *All who are struggling with broken relationships*

Some or all parts of this form of intercession may be used. Specific petitions may be added, or silence may be kept, at suitable points.

Through Christ, who ever lives to make intercession for us,
let us pray to the Lord.

Lift up our hearts to the heavenly places
and inspire us to serve you as a royal priesthood: *R*

Let all peoples acknowledge your kingdom
and grant on earth the blessing of peace: *R*

Send down upon us the gift of the Spirit
and renew your Church with power from on high: *R*

May peace abound and righteousness flourish,
that we may vanquish injustice and wrong: *R*

Help us to proclaim the good news of salvation,
and grant us the needful gifts of your grace: *R*

Let us commend the world, for which Christ prays,
to the mercy and protection of God.

Open prayer may be offered and silence is kept.

The Collect and Lord's Prayer follow.

AUTHORIZATION

Common Worship: Daily Prayer, from which this volume is drawn, is published at the request of the House of Bishops of the General Synod of the Church of England. It comprises services which comply with the provisions of A Service of the Word; material authorized for use until further resolution of the General Synod; material commended by the House of Bishops; and material, the use of which falls within the discretion allowed to the minister under the provisions of Canon B 5.

The services in this book follow the structure of A Service of the Word which is authorized pursuant to Canon B 2 of the Canons of the Church of England for use as an alternative to Morning Prayer and Evening Prayer. They are primarily intended for private use.

The obligation of the clergy under Canon C 26 to say daily the Morning and Evening Prayer is met by the use of these services, provided that in the period from the Third Sunday of Advent to the Baptism of Christ, and from Palm Sunday to Trinity Sunday, instead of the short readings provided here, the readings are taken from an authorized lectionary (such as that set out on page 39). These services may also be suitable for use in public worship, for example by groups who meet during the week, subject to the same considerations as to the choice of readings during the particular periods already referred to.

ACKNOWLEDGEMENTS

The material in this book is extracted from *Common Worship: Daily Prayer*. Thanks are due to the following for permission to reproduce copyright material:

- The Archbishops' Council of the Church of England: *Common Worship: Services and Prayers for the Church of England* which is copyright © The Archbishops' Council of the Church of England.

- The Division of Christian Education of the National Council of Churches in the USA: Scripture quotations from *The New Revised Standard Version of the Bible*, copyright © 1989 by the Division of Christian Education of the National Council of Churches in the USA. Used by permission. All rights reserved.

- The English Language Liturgical Consultation: English translation of The Lord's Prayer, Gloria Patri, Benedictus and Magnificat, prepared by the English Language Liturgical Consultation, based on (or excerpted from) *Praying Together* © ELLC, 1988.

- The European Province of the Society of St Francis: extracts adapted or excerpted from *Celebrating Common Prayer* © The Society of St Francis European Province 1992 and 1996. Used by permission.

- The Collect for Thy Kingdom Come and the Thy Kingdom Come logo are copyright © Thy Kingdom Come. Used by permission.

The Lord's Prayer

Being made one by the power of the Spirit,
as our Saviour taught us, so we pray

All **Our Father in heaven,**
hallowed be your name,
your kingdom come,
your will be done,
on earth as in heaven.
Give us today our daily bread.
Forgive us our sins
as we forgive those who sin against us.
Lead us not into temptation
but deliver us from evil.
For the kingdom, the power,
and the glory are yours
now and for ever.
Amen.

(or)

Being made one by the power of the Spirit,
let us pray with confidence as our Saviour has taught us

All **Our Father, who art in heaven,**
hallowed be thy name;
thy kingdom come;
thy will be done;
on earth as it is in heaven.
Give us this day our daily bread.
And forgive us our trespasses,
as we forgive those who trespass against us.
And lead us not into temptation;
but deliver us from evil.
For thine is the kingdom,
the power, and the glory
for ever and ever.
Amen.